Unhitched: The Book Of Jonah

How God's People Need to Connect to God's Nature

Nate Holdridge

First paperback edition October 2022

Edited by Elsa Dooling and Anne Jensen

Cover Art by BK Designs (bklingenberg.com)

Audiobook Engineering by Daniel Reed

Ebook ISBN: 9798215074152

ISBN: 9798215354711

nateholdridge.com

Contents

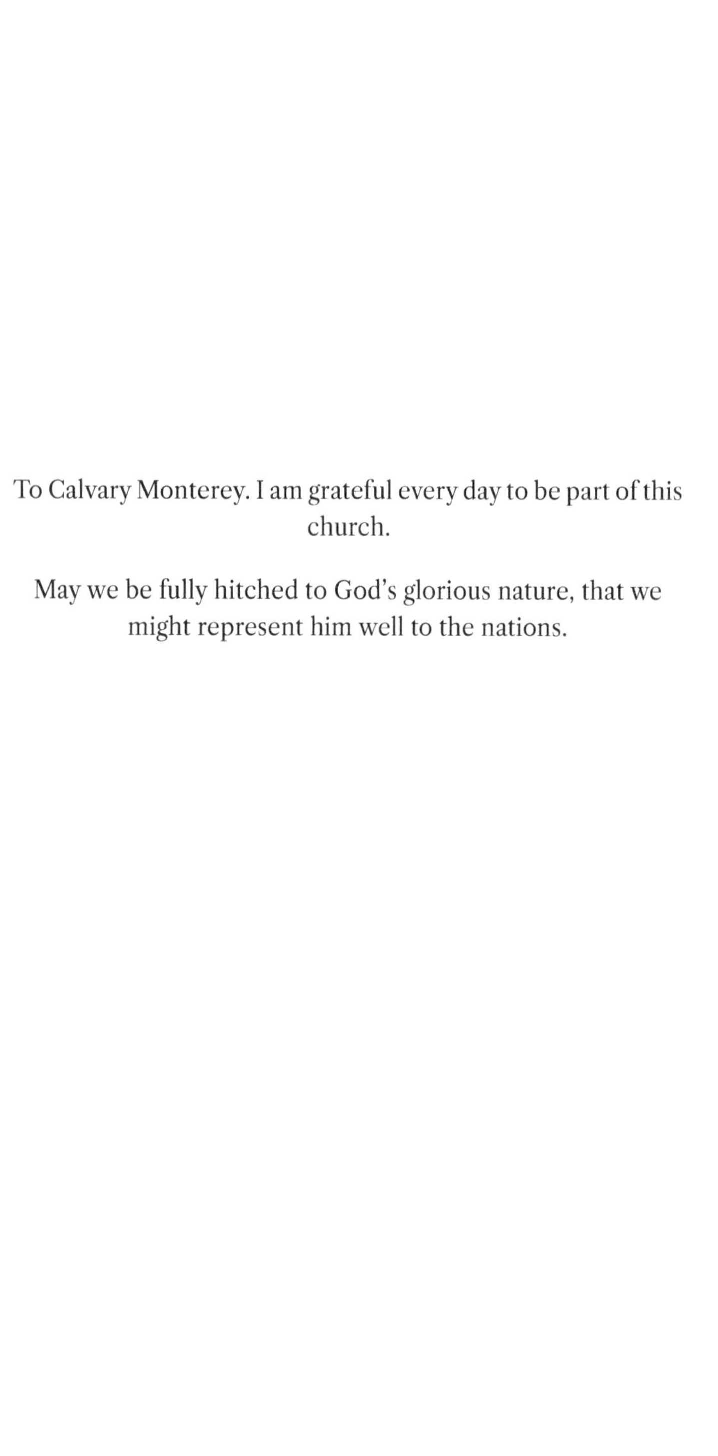

To Calvary Monterey. I am grateful every day to be part of this church.

May we be fully hitched to God's glorious nature, that we might represent him well to the nations.

God Sends (Jonah 1)

God Sends Because It's His Nature

Now the word of the LORD came to Jonah the son of Amittai, saying, "Arise, go to Nineveh, that great city, and call out against it, for their evil has come up before me." But Jonah rose to flee to Tarshish from the presence of the LORD. He went down to Joppa and found a ship going to Tarshish. So he paid the fare and went down into it, to go with them to Tarshish, away from the presence of the LORD. But the LORD hurled a great wind upon the sea, and there was a mighty tempest on the sea, so that the ship threatened to break up. Then the mariners were afraid, and each cried out to his god. And they hurled the cargo that was in the ship into the sea to lighten it for them. But Jonah had gone down

into the inner part of the ship and had lain down and was fast asleep. So the captain came and said to him, "What do you mean, you sleeper? Arise, call out to your god! Perhaps the god will give a thought to us, that we may not perish."
(Jonah 1:1–6)

We do not know much about **Jonah, the son of Amittai,** and there is precious little background material about him in the pages of Israel's history. The tiny bit we do know is that he prophesied wonderful news to King Jeroboam. After many hard, bleak years in Israel, their borders would finally be restored, and peace and prosperity would flow (2 Kings 14:25).

From this little snippet in 2 Kings, we learn Jonah had been a prophet with good news for Israel, but now he is tasked with bringing bad news to Nineveh, a city over 500 miles from Israel. In the past, he had a positive message for God's believing people, but now he is given a negative message for unbelieving people.

And this prophet did an uncharacteristic thing—at least for a prophet—he tried to run from God. Jonah decided to go to **Tarshish**, a city far away and in the opposite direction of his assignment (3).

After finding a boat that would take him as a passenger, Jonah **paid the fair** and settled in for the long journey (3). However, God would not allow his man to run for long, as he **hurled a great wind upon the sea** (4). The **tempest threatened** to **break up** the ship, so all the sailors on board grew fearful and **cried out to their gods** (5). When there was no response, the **captain** woke Jonah so he could pray to his God (6).

Some wonder if it was a false sense of peace that helped Jonah sleep through the storm. I wonder if he was simply a seasick land-lover and guilty prophet who could only cope with his mixture of seasickness and rebellion against God with mind-numbing sleep.

Why Did Jonah Run?

So why did he run? This is the major question of this first movement and a key to understanding how this book applies to us today.

Some think Jonah was fearful about what would happen to him in Nineveh. This is a reasonable explanation because Assyria was one of the cruelest and most violent empires in the world, and Nineveh was its capital. Their kings wrote boasts of atrocities and war crimes that would make you squirm in your seat. The ways they would humiliate opponents and torture their captives were legendary, and Jonah likely feared for his safety in a town like Nineveh.

Yet, this reason overlooks the rest of the book of Jonah. Jonah (spoiler alert!) eventually went to Nineveh, and everyone there repented of their evil and God relented from the judgment he had promised if they had not. When Jonah saw this, he confessed why he ran from God's will. He said:

> *O Lord, is not this what I said when I was yet in my country? That is why I made haste to flee to Tarshish; for I knew that you are a gracious God and merciful, slow to anger and abounding in steadfast love, and relenting from disaster. (Jonah 4:2)*

Jonah's reason for rebelling against God had to do with what he knew about God. Other prophets had predicted judgment on surrounding nations—*but from the safety of Israel.* Their prophecies were *about foreign nations* but were mostly *meant for Israel* to hear so they would trust God in the face of massive opponents.

But if God was *sending* Jonah to Nineveh—since God is gracious, merciful, slow to anger, and abounding in loving kindness—it probably meant that God was going to show that grace, mercy, patience, and love to Nineveh. And Jonah did not like that. He was used to telling God's people that their borders would be restored. He did not want to tell people far from God even a word of judgment, lest they repent and become God's people.

This is where I want to point out that God is a sending God because it is his nature. He sends us into the world to declare his gospel. He sent Jonah to the Ninevites. He sent his only begotten Son. God sends because it is his merciful, gracious, patient, and loving nature to do so.

But, though Jonah's theology about God was accurate, though he believed the right things about God, though he knew God was gracious, he only liked it when it applied to him and his people—not when it applied to *those* people, the Ninevites. So Jonah decided to live out his own desires rather than allow his actions to flow from what he knew of God.

This is why I have titled this book on Jonah *Unhitched.* Like a train car unhitched from the locomotive, Jonah was unhitched from God. God's heart and nature, what he stated himself to be to Moses on the top of Mt. Sinai and embedded in the Israelite Law itself, did not impact Jonah as it should. Jonah should have seen who God is and then lived in a way that represented God's nature well. Instead, he unhitched.

I almost (comically) called this book *The Caboose Is Loose* because Jonah is like the last train car, unhitching himself from following his God into the Ninevite territory.

Make no mistake: God is the main character of the book of Jonah. The book is primarily designed to teach us about him. He is mentioned twice as much as Jonah, and he is active throughout the whole story. In this first chapter, he sent Jonah. In chapter two, after Jonah is thrown overboard, God extends grace to Jonah. In chapter three, after seeing Nineveh's repentance, he responded to their prayers for mercy. And in chapter four, after tolerating Jonah's tantrum God's mercy to the Ninevites, he trained his prophet. God is the one working in this book. His man is defective, but God is not.

The big mission of God in this book was not to reach the Ninevites but to reach his people, the Israelites. Jonah knew the right things about God but did not understand the magnitude of God's grace, and the outflow was that he hated the people of Nineveh. This book was originally written for an Israelite audience who had the same difficulty understanding the grace of God that Jonah had. As God's people, they were called to be a light to the world, a kingdom of priests to a world in need of God, but they had become so insular and angry and entitled they could not fulfill their mission. They forgot how God's grace had reached them in the past and was meant to flow through them in the present. God's actions throughout the book of Jonah were meant to retrain them to let their actions better represent God's nature.

And now Christ has come and has fulfilled the Old Testament for us. The book of Jonah is now ours. We are God's people, and God's message is the same: *Understand who I am. I am gracious, merciful, slow to anger, and abounding in lovingkindness. I sent my Son to save people from their sin, and I want you to deliver this message to all nations, even if it is scary.*

God Sends His People To Represent Him

> *"And they said to one another, "Come, let us cast lots, that we may know on whose account this evil has come upon us." So they cast lots, and the lot fell on Jonah. Then they said to him, "Tell us on whose account this evil has come upon us. What is your occupation? And where do you come from? What is your country? And of what people are you?" And he said to them, "I am a Hebrew, and I fear the LORD, the God of heaven, who made the sea and the dry land." Then the men were exceedingly afraid and said to him, "What is this that you have done!" For the men knew that he was fleeing from the presence of the LORD, because he had told them." (Jonah 1:7–10)*

In this next movement, the crew, along with Jonah, **cast lots** as a method to determine the cause of this obviously supernatural storm (7). They might have passed around a bag of black rocks—whoever drew the one white rock inside was the culprit. They might have done something else; the ancients had many similar methods to try to discern the will, thoughts, or intentions of the divine.

As he does all book long, the true God flexed his sovereignty and caused the lot to fall to Jonah. Immediately, the sailors interrogated Jonah with an avalanche of questions. And all the questions had embarrassing answers.

- Q: *What is your occupation?* A: *I am one of God's prophets. We go wherever and say whatever God wants—except for this time.*

- Q: *Where do you come from?* A: *I come from Israel, the place the true God resides in his temple, the Promised Land, but I am leaving it.*

- Q: *Who are your people?* A: *We are Hebrews, God's specially called people, that we might demonstrate the true God to the lost world, but I don't want to.*

But Jonah did not back away from it. Leading with his identity as a Hebrew, Jonah revealed to them that he belonged to God but was trying to **flee from his presence** (9-10).

I have already pointed out that God is a sending God and that this action flows from his nature. And I want to add that God sends his people *so that* we might represent him well.

Jonah, of course, was not doing a good job of this. It is tempting to call a study of Jonah *"What Not To Do: Studies in the life of Jonah."* And here we have him, on the boat, amid his rebellion, telling everyone that he belongs to God. He was not a good representative of God. He had much to learn.

One major reason people give for refusing to believe in God and his gospel is hypocrisy in the church. This reminds me of a character in Moby Dick who sought to learn from Christian sailors but said that *"the practices of whalemen soon convinced him that even Christians could be both miserable and wicked; infinitely more so, than all his father's heathens."*[1]

What Should We Do?

So what are we to do? None of us can expect to always and at all times represent Jesus without error. If you have trusted him, he has given you a new nature and heart. And though this is true, we still have a body of sin to contend with, and those appetites often lead us into hypocritical actions that are inconsistent with God and his gospel.

What must we do? Strive for perfection? We cannot—perfection is impossible this side of heaven. Instead, we must be humble and contrite when we fall short. Jonah had fallen short, yet God used even his rebellion to reach people. And God might use your stories of failure and weakness to reach others if you humbly repent and show godly contrition over what you've done.

We are called to represent the Lord through our lives today by loving God and our neighbor (Luke 10:27). This love of neighbor begins with how we treat one another. Jesus said all people would know we are his disciples if we have love for one another (John 13:35).

It reminds me of a pastor friend of mine who has two elementary school-aged sons. They are energetic boys who sometimes, as pastor's kids do, get tired of waiting around for their parents after church services. One Sunday, they began playfully warring against each other in the empty church sanctuary while their parents talked to people outside. One of them picked up a Bible and threw it at the other, and it connected. He had successfully used the word of God to hurt his brother!

This reminds me of how we often treat each other, even using the Bible to attack and devour. This must not be. Love must predominate among the church and for the church because who wants to join a warring family?

We might resist this message a bit by thinking that the world has no business assessing the church. But the sailors seemed to have a right to assess Jonah's actions because they impacted them so severely, just as the disobedience of God's people has deleterious effects on the world. If the church is not what it is meant to be, the entire planet pays the price. As Jesus said:

> *In the same way, let your light shine before others so that they may see your good works and give glory to your Father who is in heaven. (Matthew 5:16)*

This seems to imply that people will assess our lives and are expected to do so. As Paul said of himself and his ministry team: *"We are ambassadors for Christ, God making his appeal through us"* (2 Corinthians 5:20). Paul's feeling was that he and his companions were representatives of God and his gospel. He wanted people to be able to read his life and come to the right conclusions about God, just as we should want our world to see our lives and conclude that God is gracious, merciful, slow to anger, and abounding in lovingkindness.

————————

God Sent Himself

"Then they said to him, "What shall we do to you, that the sea may quiet down for us?" For the sea grew more and more tempestuous. He said to them, "Pick me up and hurl me into the sea; then the sea will quiet down for you, for I know it is because of me that this great tempest has come upon you." Nevertheless, the men rowed hard to get back to dry land, but they could not, for the sea grew more and more tempestuous against them. Therefore they called out to the LORD, "O LORD, let us not perish for this man's life, and lay not on us innocent blood, for you, O LORD, have done as it pleased you." So they picked up Jonah and hurled him into the sea, and the sea ceased from its raging. Then the men feared the LORD exceedingly, and they offered a sacrifice to the LORD and made vows. And the LORD appointed a great fish to swallow up Jonah. And Jonah was in the belly of the fish three days and three nights." (Jonah 1:11–17)

In this final movement of the opening story, the sailors, having determined that Jonah is the cause of the worsening storm, asked him what they should do with him (11). Jonah told them to **pick him up** and **hurl him into the sea** (12). If they did, the sea would become calm for them.

But rather than behave as Jonah expected unbelieving Gentile sailors to behave, these men instead began **rowing hard** to get back to shore for Jonah (13). They were not bloodthirsty but instead did not want **innocent blood** to be on their hands (14). God had made them in his image and, though tainted and broken by sin, these men were living in the echo of that original creation, acting, at least at that moment, as God would have them.

Yet, when it became obvious that they had no other choice, these men prayed to God, asked for mercy, and threw Jonah overboard (14-15). When the sea immediately stopped **raging** and peace came into their lives, these men did not forget God, as many do when trials subside, but instead worshipped God (15-16).

Though the story was over for the sailors, it was not over for Jonah. God had **appointed a great fish to swallow up Jonah** (17). It was likely a large whale—ancient Hebrews kept their distance from the ocean's waters and used the same word as *fish* to describe whales. And Jonah—rather miraculously—**was in the belly of the fish** for at least part of **three days and three nights** (17).

Why Did Jonah Tell Them To Throw Him Overboard?

The great question of this movement is why did Jonah tell the sailors to throw him into the sea? Some think Jonah was still seething about his assignment to Nineveh, so he resigned himself to death. If this is true, Jonah is saying something like, *"It would be better for me to die in the Mediterranean than preach to the Ninevites. I would rather die than see them converted."*

Others think that Jonah had a major change of heart through the events of the storm. The kindness of the sailors and the magnitude of the storm may have brought him to a place of compassion. If this is true, Jonah is saying something like, *"I want you all to live, and there is only one way for that to happen. Throw me overboard. I will die instead of you."*

This second view has appeal because it reminds us of Jesus—the One who died for the many—but it forgets Jonah's attitude in the second half of his book. Even in the end, Jonah was not happy about salvation for those outside the believing community.

The truth of Jonah's attitude likely lies somewhere in the middle. This was, after all, a messy moment during a tumultuous storm. Linear, tempered, or logical thought is long gone. Jonah is likely a mix of adrenaline, fear, regret, depression, and anger—along with the recognition of what he has done to these poor sailors. He probably looked into their anxious faces and realized their humanity. But years of nationalistic enthusiasm probably also clouded his mind. Nevertheless, his conclusion was right—he had to go overboard.

Whatever Jonah's motivation, we know true love is substitutionary. Jesus loved us enough to substitute himself for us. Jonah sacrificed himself, died instead of the sailors, and in doing so, became a picture of Jesus Christ, the One who gave himself for all of humanity on the cross. Jesus even pointed this out, claiming Jonah as the perfect sign for what he was about to do:

> *...No sign will be given to (this generation) except the sign of the prophet Jonah. For just as Jonah was three days and three nights in the belly of the great fish, so will the Son of Man be*

three days and three nights in the heart of the earth. (Matthew 12:39–40)

So, yes, God sends because it is his nature to do so. Yes, God sends us to represent him. But, ultimately, God sent himself. Like Jonah, One died so that we all might live. Jesus came to our storm-tossed world and threw himself into the waves of God's wrath so we might survive.

And though Jonah became like so many of the Old Testament characters—a picture pointing forward to Jesus—the differences between him and Jesus are staggering. Jonah was cast out for his own sins; Jesus was cast out for ours. Jonah only came near death when he went under those waters; Jesus passed under the true darkness of death. Jonah was unwilling to participate in God's mission; Jesus eagerly came to earth in obedience to the Father.

For Christ, we rejoice. He is our better-than-Jonah-savior who spent three days and nights in death for us. But our passage asks us to do more than rejoice. It wants us to go, to see ourselves as sent into a broken world where—yes—evil exists everywhere. The sending God who sent himself wants to send us into it.

Joppa

When Jonah ran from God, the first place he went was the coastal town of Joppa. There, he found a ship so he could head in the opposite direction of God's will.

Centuries later, a small group of Christians gathered in a house in Joppa. Even though it had been ten years since Jesus rose from the dead, the church was still exclusively Jewish. As the group prepared lunch downstairs, the Apostle Peter was up on the rooftop portico praying to God. Then and there, he received a vision that told him to go up the coast to Caesarea and preach to a Roman army officer and his household. God was telling Peter to preach to the non-Jewish nations about Jesus.

Peter, there in Joppa, had a decision—*do I run from God's mission or allow God to send me?* Fortunately for most of us here today, Peter accepted God's invitation, and the gospel began to go to the whole world.

Joppa, the city known for Jonah's rebellion against God's plan to reach the Ninevites, became the launching pad for God's plan to reach the nations. And we are the recipients, as well as the conduits, of that mission, called to preach the gospel to our world. We are called to go because our God sends us.

---

1. Melville, Herman. 2021. Moby Dick by Herman Melville. Independently Published.

God Extends Grace (Jonah 2)

"Then Jonah prayed to the LORD his God from the belly of the fish, saying, "I called out to the LORD, out of my distress, and he answered me; out of the belly of Sheol I cried, and you heard my voice. For you cast me into the deep, into the heart of the seas, and the flood surrounded me; all your waves and your billows passed over me. Then I said, 'I am driven away from your sight; yet I shall again look upon your holy temple.' The waters closed in over me to take my life; the deep surrounded me; weeds were wrapped about my head at the roots of the mountains. I went down to the land whose bars closed upon me forever; yet you brought up my life from the pit, O LORD my God. When my life was fainting away, I remembered the LORD, and my prayer came to you, into your holy temple. Those who pay regard to vain idols forsake their hope of

steadfast love. But I with the voice of thanks-
giving will sacrifice to you; what I have vowed
I will pay. Salvation belongs to the LORD!"
And the LORD spoke to the fish, and it vomited
Jonah out upon the dry land." (Jonah 2)

In our opening chapter, we considered Jonah's background. Very little is said of him in the books of Kings and Chronicles, but what is written shows us a man who prophesied good news to Israel. He was not like many of the prophets who had to confront God's people with their sins. Instead, God used him to declare a season of peace and prosperity, a time when the borders of Israel would be restored (2 Kings 14:25).

At that time, Jonah had a positive message for God's people. Now, in the book of Jonah, the prophet has been tasked with the opposite—he has a negative message for Nineveh, people far from God.

But Jonah did not want to go. In the final episode of his story, he told God why he did not want to go—because he knew God's gracious, merciful, patient, and loving nature (Jonah 4:2). He knew that if God was *sending* him over 500 miles to preach a word of judgment to the Assyrian capital, God was desiring to withhold judgment if they repented. And Jonah did not like that. Like a train car unhitched from the locomotive, Jonah had entirely unhitched himself from God's nature. Disconnected from God's grace, Jonah turned into a legalistic and repulsive man.

Jonah needed to reconnect with God's grace, and that is what this book is about. God's goal for Jonah was that he would comprehend grace. God has the same goal for us in Jonah—he wants us to know grace.

But what is God's grace? Theologian Henry Thiessen described it as "God's goodness manifested toward the ill-deserving."[1] Elyse Fitzpatrick said grace "is God's assured favorable attitude toward undeserving rebels whom, in his inscrutable love, he has decided to bless."[2] These definitions are excellent portrayals of Jonah. He is the ill-deserving, undeserving rebel at this point of his story, but God is manifesting his goodness and inscrutable love to Jonah by rescuing him from the perils of the Mediterranean.

God's mission was to hitch Jonah up to the grace he was showing him in those waters. God needed Jonah to reconnect to his nature. He wants the same for us. He does not want us to merely have correct theology about God—*Jonah had that!*—but he wants us to live out the implications of his nature. If God is gracious, merciful, slow to anger, and abounding in loving kindness, he wants us to demonstrate the same to our world. And God will do for us what he did for Jonah in the sea—he will reach us wherever we are to give us a firm lesson on grace.

Yet to understand this passage in Jonah, we must first reject any cartoonish version of this story we have held onto in our minds. We should not picture a man diving off the edge of a boat and straight into the open mouth of a large whale. What we should imagine is a man desperately clinging to life. He is sure of death as he sinks into the storm's waters. Everything else fades away—the wind, the sailors, the boat—all of it is gone. Now, we are alone with Jonah and his thoughts.

And what we will discover along with Jonah is that God's grace is there in the depths of the ocean—and the depths of the great fish. Jonah prays a poetic psalm of thanksgiving for the grace of God's salvation. Let us inspect God's grace by inspecting Jonah's song.

God's Grace Can Be Found in the Dark

Utter Darkness

The first point I want to make is that God's grace can be found in the dark. When Jonah was cast into the sea, he was thrown into the chaos of darkness. Throughout his song, he highlighted the desperate nature of his situation. He said he was in **distress** because he was **cast into the deep** (2-3). He spoke of **waves** and **billows** and **waters** that **closed in over him to take his life** (3-5). He felt that he was at the bottom of the ocean, **the roots of the mountains**, with **bars that** were ready to **close on him forever** (6).

From our vantage point, Jonah's situation might be amusing, but it was not comedy to him. He was in the disorienting experience of drowning and dying before being swallowed by a sea creature. I do not think many of us can imagine just how wildly this would have stressed Jonah's system.

I read of one study done in the 1950s to try to understand how some prisoners of war were being turned to their captor's side by placing them in total darkness. A psychologist named Donald Hebb paid volunteers to enter "sensory isolation." He put them in small, soundproofed cells, made them wear frosted goggles that impaired their vision, and even fitted them with special gloves to decrease their sense of touch.

The result shocked the researchers: the subjects were completely disoriented after just a few hours. When they took a break to relieve themselves, they would get lost in the bathroom. One was released and immediately crashed his car. And most of them had hallucinations—they saw things like dancing squirrels and old men driving around in bathtubs or even a second version of themselves. Without the normal stream of input to their senses, each subject's brain produced its own stream of input.[3]

All this to say, Jonah was being pushed to the limits inside that fish. His senses were being brutalized through the process of drowning and then being swallowed by a large sea creature. Like the chaos of war, Jonah would have become overwhelmed as the ocean battled against him. Yet, as all his other senses were submerged in the water, his spiritual senses rose to the surface. The man who did not think of God while in the storm began realizing his deep need for Him.

Stripped of Everything But God

It was as if Jonah was stripped of everything but God. To Jonah, everything else was dead. He felt he was in **Sheol**, the place of the dead (2). But, in the darkness, a ray of light began to shine.

I think this is why Jonah said, near the end of his song, that **those who pay regard to vain idols forsake their hope of steadfast love** (8). I do not think Jonah was referring to the idolatry of the sailors or the Ninevites. Jonah had made an idol of his perception of good and evil, righteousness and unrighteousness. He might have even made an idol of his identity as a Hebrew. Alone in the sea, Jonah saw how he had built an idol out of his perspective on himself and the Ninevites. He realized that his idolatrous heart meant the **steadfast love** of God could not do its beautiful work in his heart. So God put him in the fish in the ocean to strip all of those idols from his life.

The first of the ten commandments says, "You shall have no other gods before me" (Exodus 20:3, ESV). As Tim Keller says, "An idol is whatever you look at and say, in your heart of hearts, 'If I have that, then I'll feel my life has meaning, then I'll know I have value, then I'll feel significant and secure.'"[4]

Down in that fish, Jonah came to terms with his worship. He saw how he had worshiped ideas and principles out of step with God. He realized he had thought of his hatred of the Ninevites as more core to his identity than his connection to God. Who and what he was against meant more to him than the God who was for him. And, as he realized his idolatry, he began sensing God's steadfast love warming his soul once again.

As God stripped away Jonah's idols, showing him how foolish they were and how little they could do for him, Jonah saw God again. In the dark, Jonah began enjoying God again.

Recently, a woman named Laura Young bought a two-thousand-year-old Roman bust—they think it is of the man who killed Julius Caesar. She found it on sale at an Austin, Texas Goodwill for thirty-five dollars. A collector of antiques, she knew it was worth much more than that. Obviously, Goodwill and whoever donated it to them did not. Now, this piece is sitting in a museum where anyone can appreciate its value.

There are times in our lives when God is like that Roman bust sitting on a shelf in Goodwill—undervalued and under-appreciated. And sometimes God will allow darkness to come into our lives as a way to get us to see what is truly valuable. God is not meant to be a cheap accessory to our lives but the very center of who we are. Only he can bear the weight of our worship, so we must value him higher than anyone or anything.

Jonah found grace in the darkness and was illuminated by it. But Jonah, in the belly of the fish, felt he was dead and had descended into the **belly of** hell, but he was not and had not (2). The **bars**, as he said, had not **closed upon him forever** (6).

As intense as his grief was at that moment, Jesus Christ entered into a state of darkness, death, and forsakenness Jonah could never know. When Jesus died on the cross, he experienced separation from the Father. That is what hell is—total separation from God (2 Thessalonians 1:9). The Bible uses images like fire and darkness to describe it, but at the end of the day, hell is existence completely away and apart from God. And Jesus endured that separation for us while on the cross, all so that we could be reunited with the wonderful and entirely undeserved favor of God.

God's Grace Illuminates Us Without Crushing Us

Acceptance of God's Methods

Grace can be found in the dark, but grace also illuminates us without crushing us. What do I mean?

All through the song, it is clear Jonah understood that the storm, the sea, and the whale were all under God's control. He sent the wind. He manipulated the cast a lot. He prepared the great fish. Jonah said, **"You cast me into the deep, into the heart of the seas, all your waves and your billows passed over me** (3).

And, from Jonah, there is no argument- as if he has realized all he had coming to him. He has sensed the gravity of his rebellion and sin. The hard-hearted prophet who thought he knew better than God is now softened by God's grace. He realized that God's discipline was also God's rescue. Yes, the storm and the sea and the fish were all uncomfortable, but they were also necessary vehicles God was using to drive Jonah back into his loving arms.

And Jonah began growing in hope while inside the fish. He sang of going back to God's **temple** (4, 7). He did not feel it was too late to return to God, that he was somehow beyond God's grace. He saw his error and realized his need for judgment but knew God was not done with him. God was raising up his rebel. Grace had shown Jonah his error but had not decimated him. He believed he had a future and hope in and with God.

Jonah's self-righteousness had evaporated at this moment. God was birthing something new within his man. He was no longer pompous and proud but humble and contrite. He knew he deserved judgment but had instead received God's grace.

As Jerry Bridges wrote: *"Your worst days are never so bad that you are beyond the reach of God's grace."*[5]

This is the Christian perspective. God upholds us when we are at our worst. In the dark, illuminated by God, we are not crushed by God. Contrast this with the mindset of the world. William McRaven's short book *Make Your Bed* is filled with many great insights. At one point, he said, *"We will all confront a dark moment in life...In that dark moment, reach deep inside yourself and be your very best."*[6]

But what do we do when we are the *cause* of the dark moment? What happens when we reach inside ourselves and discern it is a place where no good dwells? It is there that we must know that we are not beyond the reach of God's grace. I cannot say this enough: you are not beyond the reach of God's grace. If Jonah shows us nothing else, he shows us God does not give up. He keeps reaching out to his own.

———

God's Grace Produces a Beautiful Response

Response!

The last element of God's grace I want you to see from this passage is that it produces a beautiful response. When God's grace truly impacts your heart—when you realize the magnitude of his mercy and kindness toward you—you cannot help but respond.

I am firmly convinced by the idea that an understanding of God's grace, no matter how small that understanding is, can have major results. I believe human life becomes most human when it is lived in light of God's grace. Grace is a producer, and this is a major reason the church I pastor has a vision statement of *Jesus Famous.*

Jesus brought God's grace—his cross gave God's favor access to us. Like a dam blown up by dynamite so that the old river can flow again, Christ's cross blew up sin, the obstacle to God's grace flowing in our lives. The more appreciative of Christ you become—the more Jesus becomes famous to you—the more grace-driven you will become. Grace will produce!

Consider how Paul described the response-producing nature of God's grace:

> *For the grace of God has appeared that offers salvation to all people. It teaches us to say "No" to ungodliness and worldly passions, and to live self-controlled, upright and godly lives in this present age, while we wait for the blessed hope—the appearing of the glory of our great God and Savior, Jesus Christ, who gave himself for us to redeem us from all wickedness and to purify for himself a people that are his very own, eager to do what is good. (Titus 2:11–14, NIV)*

What is Paul saying? God's grace teaches us to live holy lives. God's grace is the motivation *to live self-controlled, upright, and godly lives in this present age.* It is God's grace that produces a *people* who are *eager to do what is good*. As God's grace is taught, we will respond in the best of ways.

So how did Jonah respond?

Renewed Relationship With God

Jonah responded by renewing his relationship with God. You probably noticed throughout his psalm that his walk with God was rekindled while there in the darkness of the fish. From there, he **called out to the Lord**, directing his prayers to God's heavenly temple (2, 4, 7, 9). He might have received his original mission from God while sacrificing to God in Jerusalem's temple, but now he is so far from God's temple, inside a stinking fish, yet his connection to his Father in heaven is stronger than ever. He might have tried to run from God's presence, but now he is running to his God.

And he did not stop with prayer. He went on to devote himself to God again. He said, **"I with the voice of thanksgiving will sacrifice to you; what I have vowed I will pay"** (9). Jonah was saying he would go again to the temple, give God a thanksgiving offering, and dedicate himself to God with that offering. It was a prayer of dedication and commitment—marks of a true revival in Jonah's heart. He might have run from God, but now he reenlists with God.

We do not offer animal sacrifices as a way to dedicate ourselves to God. Instead, we offer ourselves as living sacrifices:

> *And so, dear brothers and sisters, I plead with you to give your bodies to God because of all he*

> *has done for you. Let them be a living and holy sacrifice—the kind he will find acceptable. This is truly the way to worship him. (Romans 12:1, NLT)*

Jonah did this. He spoke of sacrifices in the temple, but his life would be a sacrifice also. Jonah knew his commitment to God, his vow, would require him to obediently go and preach to Nineveh. He knew his sacrifice would cost him, but God's grace drove him back into devotion to God.

Recognition of Salvation's Source

Jonah also responded to God's grace with a shout of praise: **"Salvation belongs to the Lord!"** (9). It was a statement of recognition—God saved the sailors. God saved Jonah. And God would save Nineveh. He saves.

It was also a statement of submission—God can give salvation to whomever he chooses. Jonah had stubbornly acted as if he was the arbiter of salvation, but God had shown him he was wrong to take that position. God decides.

And it was also a statement intermixed with tension. There, in the fish, during a song, Jonah is ready to confess that salvation belongs to the Lord. *You can save who you want, O God. You can reach into lives I have deemed too evil for your grace. You can rescue anyone!* But this is not the end of Jonah's story. We already considered the end, how he would go to Nineveh, preach, and then be angered when God withholds his judgment from them. He certainly was not singing about how salvation belonged to the Lord then.

All this might lead us to think that Jonah's encounter with God's grace inside the fish was not legitimate. But do not the complexities in Jonah remind us of ourselves? We humans vacillate wildly between revelation and blindness, love and anger, grace and law. Jonah, in the fish, had seen that salvation belongs to the Lord, but, once in Nineveh, his eyes became clouded. This tension within Jonah should remind us that we need constant exposure to God's grace.

When cancer is treated with chemotherapy, multiple rounds are required. One exposure will not kill the cancer. And our hard hearts require ongoing rounds of God's grace, which is part of the reason we need church gatherings, worship songs, sermons, and small groups—each gives us another exposure to grace.

Jonah became a recipient of God's grace. He went into the dark, and God was there. He realized God was not done with him, that he would again visit God's temple, and that salvation belongs to the Lord.

If only we could grow in our understanding of God's grace. Like Jonah, we need to know it for ourselves. And, also like Jonah, we need to realize it for others. Grace makes life worth living!

"Grace transforms desolate and bleak plains into rich, green pastures. It changes grit-your-teeth duty into loving, enthusiastic service. It exchanges the tears and guilt of our own failed efforts for the eternal thrill and laughter of freely offered pleasures at the right hand of God. Grace changes everything!"[7]

1. Thiessen, Henry C. 2007. Lectures in Systematic Theology. Grand Rapids, MI: William B Eerdmans Publishing.

2. Fitzpatrick, Elyse M., and Jessica Thompson. 2011. Give Them Grace: Dazzling Your Kids with the Love of Jesus. Wheaton, IL: Crossway Books.

3. Hunt, Will. 2019. "What Happens When Humans Spend Too Much Time in the Dark." Popular Science. February 1, 2019. https://www.popsci.com/sensory-deprivation-effects-darkness/.

4. Keller, Timothy J. 2009. Counterfeit Gods. Dutton Books.

5. Bridges, Jerry. 2006. The Discipline of Grace Study Guide: God's Role and Our Role in the Pursuit of Holiness. Colorado Springs, CO: NavPress.

6. McRaven, William H. 2017. Make Your Bed: Little Things That Can Change Your Life... And Maybe the World. London, England: Grand Central Publishing.

7. Smith, Chuck. 2008. Why Grace Changes Everything. Word for Today.

3

God Is Compassionate (Jonah 3)

The second half of the book of Jonah is similar to the first. Both halves begin with God telling Jonah to go and preach in Nineveh. Both halves go on to describe Jonah's interactions with nonbelievers from outside Israel, first with the sailors on the boat and then with the citizens of Nineveh. And both halves conclude with Jonah talking to God—first from the belly of the fish and then from the outskirts of Nineveh.

And this second half of Jonah is a second chance for Jonah. Like he had done for Abraham and Moses and David and Peter, God gave Jonah an opportunity after failure. And—at least at first glance—it does not end well.

But Jonah was in God's school, relearning his God. And in this next episode, Jonah learns that the predominant attribute of God is his loving compassion. To a degree, the prophet knew of God's compassion, but God's nature needed to seep into Jonah's. Even though God had shown him amazing grace and steadfast love in the belly of the fish, Jonah struggled to embrace God's grace and love for others. Jonah was unhitched from what he knew about the gracious, merciful, patient, and loving God—and God was doing all he could to reconnect his man (Jonah 4:2).

Jonah's story is designed to get us to connect our lives and actions to God's nature as well. What is God like? The answer should inform the way we live. And in this third major movement of Jonah, we discover that God is compassionate. Jonah told God he knew of him as one who "relents from disaster," and that is precisely what God will do here (Jonah 4:2). But how does God's compassion work?

<hr>

So He Warns

Then the word of the Lord came to Jonah the second time, saying, "Arise, go to Nineveh, that great city, and call out against it the message that I tell you." So Jonah arose and went to Nineveh, according to the word of the Lord. Now Nineveh was an exceedingly great city, three days' journey in breadth. Jonah began to go into the city, going a day's journey. And he called out, "Yet forty days, and Nineveh shall be overthrown!" (Jonah 3:1–4)

In an episode about God's compassion, it might seem odd to consider the beginning. God sent his prophet into town to declare a (very) brief word of judgment: **"Yet forty days, and Nineveh shall be overthrown"** (4). Eight words in English, but only five in Hebrew.

We immediately wonder if there was more to Jonah's message. Did he give them any additional words of hope? Did he instruct them to repent? Did he unpack his short prediction so they could know how to apply it?

The passage does not give us direct answers to our questions. But there are some clues that Jonah's message might have consisted of more than a mere announcement that they were doomed.

- First, there is God's description of the city as **an exceedingly great city** (3). It is a remark about Nineveh's size, but the original language could mean *a great city to God.*[1] And though many modern believers have a hard time with city culture and life, God will show Jonah that he had a special place in his heart for this large city (Jonah 4:11).

- The second clue this message might have pointed to the possibility of forgiveness is the **forty-day** timeline Jonah gives them (4). It is not hard to imagine how someone might interpret that as a forty-day window to turn from the evil they were engaged in.

- A third clue is found in the final word of the message—**"overthrown"** (4). Nineveh understood this as a warning, but many scholars have pointed out that this word has a dual meaning in Scripture—it can mean to be "overturned in destruction" or "turned by repentance." And the Ninevites seemed to think there was a glimmer of hope that God had said it in this way.

- The final clue I will mention is that they eventually repented of their violence, which might indicate that Jonah specifically preached against it (8).

Perhaps Jonah said a bit more than is mentioned here? It is also possible they came under the conviction of the Spirit without Jonah's help; it is not hard to imagine Jonah declaring the bare minimum. Either way, the emphasis of the text is that God sent Nineveh a stark and clear message of warning.

When we think of God's compassion, the fact that he warns might not be the first element that comes to mind. Many think of these warnings in Scripture as threats—as if God could turn off his holiness and allow evil, sin, and guilt to somehow go unpunished if he wanted to. He cannot. His nature is to vanquish all that is broken and evil and unholy forever. He aims to remove it—but he does not do that abruptly, without any warning. Instead, he graciously sends messengers who alert us to impending doom.

Jonah's prophetic word is less like the loud threatening of a schoolyard bully and more like the warnings posted around a power plant. There is righteous power within God, and the Ninevites had been so cruel for so long that they would now be shocked by his judgment. But God was willing to warn them, and the warning was meant to produce repentance.

At the end of this episode, God will unleash his compassion on the Ninevites and withhold this judgment. But not before they first repented of their crimes. And for them to repent of their crimes, they needed to hear a warning judgment. We do not even know why they were so ready to hear it—some wonder if recent natural disasters or some of their spiritual practices opened them up to an oracle from a figure like Jonah. We are not told why they responded, but we should see the importance of the warning. It was step one.

This warning element is a major reason we are often shy to share the good news—the gospel—of Christ. We know it is good news because of the bad news. It is good news with a warning. Just as access to chemotherapy is good news to those with some forms of cancer, so the gospel is a joy because of our broken and lost condition. Without God's salvation, we are doomed to a forever without God. It might be forty days from now, it might be forty years from now, but unless we receive Christ, judgment is coming. And this bad news is often uncomfortable for us to share, but it is part of God's compassion, to tell the truth to a broken humanity.

So He Waits

And the people of Nineveh believed God. They called for a fast and put on sackcloth, from the greatest of them to the least of them. The word reached the king of Nineveh, and he arose from his throne, removed his robe, covered himself with sackcloth, and sat in ashes. And he issued a proclamation and published through Nineveh, "By the decree of the king and his nobles: Let neither man nor beast, herd nor flock, taste anything. Let them not feed or drink water, but let man and beast be covered with sackcloth, and let them call out mightily to God. Let everyone turn from his evil way and from the violence that is in his hands. Who knows? God may turn

and relent and turn from his fierce anger, so that
we may not perish." (Jonah 3:5–9)

The Anti-Jonah

Jonah began declaring God's message, **and the people of Nineveh believed God** (5). It is the same way Abraham's belief was described, and he is considered the father of faith (Genesis 15:6, Romans 4:3). I mention this because some wonder if Nineveh's repentance was legitimate. In later years, their society reverted to its evil practices. Later Jewish prophets cried out against Nineveh when they did, so some have wondered if the revival described here was genuine. Jesus seemed to think so:

> *"The men of Nineveh will rise up at the judg-*
> *ment with this generation and condemn it, for*
> *they repented at the preaching of Jonah, and*
> *behold, something greater than Jonah is here."*
> (Luke 11:32)

And what radical repentance it was! It began with **the people** (5). This was not a legislated morality from the top down. They did not have to pass laws that hindered people from doing evil. It all started with the populace before making its way up to the king/governor of Nineveh. Everyone clothed themselves with garments that symbolized mourning and contrition.

And once the king did hear about it, he issued a proclamation for everyone to stop what they were doing. He wanted everyone to **call out mightily to God** (8). His thought: **"Who**

knows? God may turn and relent and turn from his fierce anger, so that we may not perish" (9). He even made the city's livestock wear sackcloth, which was perhaps the equivalent of flying our flags at half-mast or painting our funeral cars black.

Why did they respond in this way? Perhaps, as I mentioned earlier, Jonah had said more than the words recorded in this chapter. But one thing is certain: God was moving in the people of Nineveh.

God produced this massive revival. God was, as Paul said in 2 Timothy, *"granting them repentance leading to a knowledge of the truth"* (2 Timothy 2:25). God was at work in their midst, giving them hope that he might turn from his anger. And God was waiting—at least forty days—for them to turn.

In *A Christmas Carol* by Charles Dickens, when the Ghost of Christmas Yet To Come showed Ebenezer Scrooge his lonely future, Scrooge says:

> *"Men's courses will foreshadow certain ends, to which, if persevered in, they must lead. But if the courses be departed from, the ends will change. Say it thus with what you show me."*[2]

He hoped he could change course and experience a different outcome. It seems the Ninevites were hoping for the same. Fortunately for them (and us), God's nature is to respond when we repent. Notice what God said through the prophet Jeremiah:

> *"If at any time I declare concerning a nation or
> a kingdom, that I will pluck up and break down
> and destroy it, and if that nation, concerning
> which I have spoken, turns from its evil, I will
> relent of the disaster that I intended to do to it."*
> (Jeremiah 18:7–8)

God is saying, "Here is something unchangeable in me. I will warn, but when people repent, I respond. It is who I am." And this hope that God would reverse course drove the Ninevites to reverse their own course. As one author said, *"The hearts of the violent can be overthrown by the mere possibility of God's compassion."*[3]

But we must note two facets of their repentance. First, everyone in the story is opposite Jonah. Consider the king. When Jonah was told to declare God's judgment in Nineveh, his first reaction was to arise, hop into a boat, get under the covers, and go to sleep. When the king heard of God's judgment, he **arose**, **removed his robe**, **covered himself with sackcloth** and **sat in ashes** (6). He did the opposite of Jonah.

Now, consider the people. With only one prophet who spoke a (very) brief prophecy, they responded with zeal. When God gave Jonah (very) clear directions, Jonah did not obey God as they did. He did the opposite of the people. Nineveh and the king's obedience were a rebuke to Jonah.

It is possible this was also a rebuke to Israel. They had many prophets and an entire Bible of revelation from God, but they often wandered from him.

And perhaps the Ninevites' response is meant to sting us a little as well. We have our leather-bound Bibles, Bible applications on our phones, and more free resources to understand

and apply the Bible than any generation in the history of humanity. But what are we doing with that understanding?

A Colony of Heaven

I also want you to notice what their repentance produced. They turned from the **violence in their hands** (8). This is important—Jonah preached the truth, and they responded by refusing to treat others violently any longer.

Some churches make the mistake of only emphasizing one and not the other. So some will emphasize serving the community, feeding the hungry, and sheltering the poor, while others will emphasize preaching the truth of the word. But both the preaching of the truth and the pursuit of a biblical version of justice are required. The truth of the word should lead to transformed lives that seek to transform the world. When we live this way, we are living out our new citizenship in heaven (Philippians 3:20). We are operating as *"a colony of heaven in a country of death."*[4]

So, as God waited, the Ninevites did what God wants every generation and people group to do—they **called** upon him (8). What did God do?

So He Responds

*When God saw what they did, how they turned
from their evil way, God relented of the disaster
that he had said he would do to them, and he
did not do it. (Jonah 3:10)*

God's Nature

God noted the response of the Ninevites to Jonah's meager preaching. As they **turned from their evil way**, **God relented of the disaster he said he would do** (10).

Some, knowing God is immutable (or cannot change), see a problem with how God behaved here. They cannot see past the anthropomorphic language—these human terms are an attempt to describe the actions of a majestic God. Some even take passages like this one and teach that God has not sovereignly set the future according to his will.

But I have already highlighted the Jeremiah 18 passage where God stated that he would not judge a nation he had promised to judge if they repented (Jeremiah 18:7-8). This seems to be the implied nature of his judgment—*it does not have to be!*

God is not changing here; he is the same yesterday, today, and forever (Hebrews 13:8). But Nineveh was changing in relation to God. Because of their repentance, they had shifted from being under God's judgment to "under God's unchanging love and forgiveness." Just as shifting from one side of a pillar to another changes your view of the pillar but does not change the pillar, so Nineveh's shift changed their experience of God, but not God himself.[5]

What this passage seems to show us is that God's overriding and primary attribute is compassion. Yes, he is righteous, so warnings of judgment must come. But when people respond to those warnings with repentance, God's compassion kicks in. It is beautiful compassion, one that dances harmoniously with his wrath inside his holiness. In our modern time, many have wanted a compassionate God who is spineless and permissive. That is not compassion; that is a jellyfish.

Juli Slattery said it well: *"Instead of worshiping a God of compassion, we have made compassion a god unto itself, ignoring God's call to righteousness and holiness. I can be moved by compassion to excuse and condone almost any sin."*[6] And people often do—even in the name of Christ—they will approve of sins God clearly denounces in his word and in the general revelation of the cosmos. But God's compassion is not an impotent weakness that settles for life as it is but a powerful force that can transform the willing.

God Saves?

God saved the Ninevite people because of his compassionate love. As Jonah confessed during his prayer in the belly of the fish, "salvation belongs to the Lord" (Jonah 2:9). And God saves because he is driven by compassion.

Some might object that all God did in this episode was save the Ninevite people from himself. He sent his prophet with a message of doom, and God saved the city from that doom when they repented. So God was only saving them from himself.

In one sense, the assessment that God was only saving Nineveh from himself is untrue. When God pronounces judgment as he did through Jonah, it is a declaration of what sin is already doing to people. God would overthrow them, which is exactly what their violence was *already* doing from within. There is no way that Assyrian society could have endured for many more generations—their manner of life was so violent and brutal that it was killing them slowly. Their toxic way of life was destroying them already, and God's forty-day timeline merely expedited the process.

Yet, in another sense, the assessment that God saved Nineveh from himself is true. As a holy and righteous God, God is rightly angered by humanity's sinful actions. The Bible teaches that his slow and long-suffering anger is stored up against all evil. He will destroy it all because he is—in a pure and righteous way—angry about it. So, in one sense, God saved Nineveh from himself when, in his compassion, he relented from his judgment.

God does the same today. Cultures and societies have chosen ways of living that are slowly killing those cultures and societies. Just as ancient Rome died from within, so modern societies are dying a long death because of the philosophies on which they are built. This long death is God's judgment. As Paul wrote, *"The wrath of God is being revealed from heaven against all the godlessness and wickedness of people"* (Romans 1:18a, NIV). It *is being revealed*. Look around; a society without God eventually burns from within.

And God does more than institute this long death. The compassionate forgiveness of God is available to us because he sent his Son to die in our place. The Son gladly embraced this mission, and because he died for our sins while he himself was completely sinless, and because he rose from the dead, all who believe in him can be cleansed by him. God came to die, not for the good people, the best people, or the perfect people, but for you and me. If you trust Christ, the Father will see you as he sees himself.

In the book and movie *The Green Mile*, John Coffey is a wrongfully accused inmate on death row.[7] But he has a supernatural gift. Through human contact, he can take in the sickness or disease of others by transferring it to someone else or taking it on himself, which he often does. To take it on himself causes him to convulse in great pain. He can help, but not without great personal cost.

Well, a greater one than John Coffey has come. He rescued us through great personal cost. God's compassion cost him dearly. Because he is holy, he could not merely dismiss our guilt. If he did that, he would be in denial of his very nature—he cannot let evil and sin exist unjudged. But his compassion drove him to judge it by consuming it in his own body on the cross. There was no one else to pass the judgment to—it was either himself or us. And he chose himself.

---

1   Bruckner, James. 2010. Jonah, Nahum, Habakkuk, Zephaniah. Kentwood, MI: Zondervan.

2. Dickens, Charles. 2009. A Christmas Carol. London, England: Vintage Classics.

3. Bruckner, James. 2010. Jonah, Nahum, Habakkuk, Zephaniah. Kentwood, MI: Zondervan.

4. Peterson, Eugene H. 2013. Practice Resurrection. Grand Rapids, MI: William B Eerdmans Publishing.

5. Geisler, Norman L., and Douglas E. Potter. 2016. A Popular Survey of Bible Doctrine. North Charleston, SC: Createspace Independent Publishing Platform.

6. Slattery, Juli. 2018. Rethinking Sexuality: God's Design and Why It Matters. Sisters, OR: Multnomah Press.

7. King, Stephen. 1996. The Green Mile. Demco Media.

4

God Trains (Jonah 4)

Finally, we come to the conclusion of Jonah's story—a conclusion many, unfortunately, forget, thinking his story is merely one about a massive storm, a big fish, and a sweeping revival. But the storm, fish, and revival were all designed to get Jonah right to this moment—for his benefit, but also for the benefit of every reader of Jonah.

This final chapter and episode in Jonah's story is important because it shows us that God is willing to patiently train his people, just as he patiently trained his prophet. If Jonah has been in God's school up to this point, this last movement is finals week. Jonah had an imbalanced understanding of God and his loves were disordered, so God descends in this final episode in an attempt to right Jonah's ship.

And God will do the same for us. When our view of him or our priorities are off, God will faithfully do what he can to train us, just as he trained his prophet thousands of years ago. So let's read the finale to Jonah's story with a consciousness that

God is also faithful to confront and shape us when needed, especially about the very issues Jonah dealt with in this story.

———

When Our Understanding Is Imbalanced

But it displeased Jonah exceedingly, and he was angry. And he prayed to the Lord and said, "O Lord, is not this what I said when I was yet in my country? That is why I made haste to flee to Tarshish; for I knew that you are a gracious God and merciful, slow to anger and abounding in steadfast love, and relenting from disaster. Therefore now, O Lord, please take my life from me, for it is better for me to die than to live." (Jonah 4:1–3)

Ongoing Argument

The first thing we note is that God is willing to train us when our understanding of him is imbalanced. We have been leading up to and commenting on this throughout our study of Jonah. Like a train car unhitched from the engine, Jonah was unhitched from what he knew about God. He was orthodox in his belief about God but unorthodox in his behavior. When it came to the way he treated the Ninevites, Jonah did not reflect God's heart at all, and this opening scene shows us why.

After Nineveh turns to God for mercy, Jonah is **exceedingly displeased** that God relented from the disaster he said he'd bring upon the Ninevites (1). But why did this displease Jonah so intensely?

- Jonah probably felt Assyria was a threat to his own nation, but it isn't the main reason he was angry.

- Jonah probably didn't want to return to Israel as *that* prophet, the one who instigated a revival among Israel's rivals, but it isn't the main reason he was angry.

- It's possible Jonah was angered that God would withhold judgment from immoral people before they had a chance to learn how to become moral—his way of obsessing over pure doctrine—but it's not the main reason he was angry.

No, Jonah tells God why he's **angry** (1-2). It was an argument he had against God since the beginning of the book when he was still **in his country** (2). He knew God was full of grace, mercy, patience, and love—and that he would try to find a way to **relent from disaster** (2). And this drove Jonah crazy, so he asked God to kill him—what a wild prayer!

Jonah, the prophet, is angry God allowed a massive revival in Nineveh. This would be like a musician who is angered that they are now the most listened to artist in the world or an athlete angered by winning a world championship. Jonah was used mightily by God—and prophets should be all about that—but he hated it because he didn't like God's gracious, merciful, and loving side.

Selective Reading

This is even hinted at in what Jonah said about God. When he said God was gracious, merciful, slow to anger, abounding in lovingkindness, and relenting from disaster, he was quoting Scripture. Seven times, the Old Testament described God the way Jonah did, starting with the time God put Moses in the cleft of the rock and broadcast his name to his man (Exodus 34:6-7).

But Jonah's description lacked a key feature—at the end of the attributes Jonah listed, in the original passage with Moses, God said he would "keep steadfast love for thousands, forgiving iniquity and transgression and sin, but who will by no means clear the guilty, visiting the iniquity of the fathers on the children and the children's children, to the third and the fourth generation." (Exodus 34:7).

This last phrase about how God would *"by no means clear the guilty"* is a necessary part of God's nature. God is prone to love, grace, forgiveness, and mercy. God is faithful to keep his covenant with us. And he is also the just God who cannot merely overlook sin. As Dane Ortland wrote:

> *"Without (this statement), all that came before (God's mercy, grace, patience, love, and for-giveness) might be understood as mere leniency."*[1]

So Jonah's accusation is clear. He thinks God is too lenient and out of balance—that he's all grace, mercy, and love—so he doesn't even mention that part of God's nature. Because Jonah lived in the real world with real evil, he chafed at the idea God would merely turn his face from all that wickedness. He did not understand how God could go around doing what he just did for the Ninevites and still be holy and just, so he refused to mention God's justice when recounting who God is.

In Jonah's mind, God is too soft, evil should be punished, and Nineveh needed to be destroyed. In Jonah's mind, people need to trust that there is a consistent God who has an order to things. And, as Tim Keller said, "In Jonah's mind, the issue is a theological one. There seems to be a contradiction between the justice of God and the love of God."[2] He probably feared that news of what God did for Nineveh would get out—pretty soon, no one would think twice about evil because God is so gracious!

But Jonah's imbalanced understanding of God—his inability to see how God's love and justice, grace and holiness were not at odds with one another—was made worse by an improper ordering of Jonah's loves.

It is true that we sometimes love the wrong things—such was the case with the forbidden fruit of the garden and the forbidden sins of life today. When a person cheats on their spouse, for instance, they are loving the wrong things. But there are also times when we love lesser things more than we ought and greater things less than we should. When a person loves their career more than God, for instance, they are loving a lesser thing more than a greater thing.

But God is faithful amid our seasons of unfaithfulness, and part of his faithfulness is his ongoing patience in training us to love correctly. He works hard to reorder our loves. This is how Jonah's story concludes—God worked to reorder Jonah's loves.

When Our Loves Are Disordered

And the Lord said, "Do you do well to be angry?" Jonah went out of the city and sat to the east of the city and made a booth for himself there. He sat under it in the shade, till he should see what would become of the city. Now the Lord God appointed a plant and made it come up over Jonah, that it might be a shade over his head, to save him from his discomfort. So Jonah was exceedingly glad because of the plant. But when dawn came up the next day, God appointed a worm that attacked the plant, so that it withered. When the sun rose, God appointed a scorching east wind, and the sun beat down on the head of Jonah so that he was faint. And he asked that he might die and said, "It is better for me to die than to live." But God said to Jonah, "Do you do well to be angry for the plant?" And he said, "Yes, I do well to be angry, angry enough to die." (Jonah 4:4–9)

God Counsels Jonah

Not only does God patiently train us when our understanding of him is imbalanced, but also when our loves are disordered. Here, Jonah's inner arguments against God have bubbled to the surface, but now God takes Jonah into his counseling office. He puts Jonah on the couch and prepares a devastating lesson for his prophet. It started when Jonah went out to the **east of the city till he should see what would become of the city** (5). Rather than disciple all the new believers in Nineveh, Jonah hoped God would relent from his relenting and rain down judgment on the people. He even made a **booth for himself** so he could wait...and wait...and wait.

But Jonah's ramshackle booth was no match for the heat of that region, so God (once again) manipulated nature to train his man by sending a plant to come up **over Jonah so that it might be a shade over his head, to save him from his discomfort** (6). Jonah was really **glad** to have the plant and was really angry when God sent a **worm** to **attack the plant**, followed by a **scorching east wind** to pummel Jonah (7-8). Jonah was so distraught that he said—to no one in particular—**"It is better for me to die than to live"** (8). God asked him, again, if it was right for him to be **angry** (9). Defiantly, Jonah said, **"Yes, I do well to be angry, angry enough to die"** (9).

Wow.

Jonah is clearly a mixture within. In the belly of the fish, he rejoiced over God's grace. Here, in the scorching sun, he despaired of life. The lessons he had learned halfway through his book seemed to have evaporated with the heat of high noon and were blown away by the brutal eastern wind. Through it all, God asked, "Do you do well to be angry?"

Jonah's Love

Jonah's loves are on full display in this closing story. We are told that, when the plant appeared, Jonah **was exceedingly glad** (6). It is a particularly strong phrase meant to communicate that Jonah was ecstatic over this plant. He was doing cartwheels in joy over this development in his life. But for as super-pumped as he was for the plant's existence, he was equally demoralized when it was removed and he became intensely uncomfortable.

Jonah's emotions displayed his loves for all to see. Clearly, Jonah was in love with his own comfort. And, though we might expect him to appreciate a plant that shielded him from the elements—and also get a bit cranky when he is delivered over to the heat of the sun—God's point is not that Jonah *shouldn't* have cared about these things. *It's that Jonah should have cared less about them and more about the right things.*

Clearly, Jonah cared so much more for his personal comfort than he did for the saving of the lost souls of Nineveh—that was the reality deep down in Jonah's heart. He cared more for Israel's comfort and safety than he did for Assyria's conversion. Of course, he cared about his own people—that's normal. But his loves were so disordered that he buried his love for his neighbor underneath his love for himself.

What about us? Where and why and how are we angered? And do those moments of anger reveal that we are often more concerned with our own peace, prosperity, and comfort than we are with the lost? And when we are frustrated that the world and its systems do not reflect Christ and his values, are we upset about it because we are concerned for people's souls or because we just don't like having to figure out how to live as a religious minority?

So God has questioned Jonah twice about his anger, but now he asks him one final question. It is the question that clinches God's argument:

> *And the Lord said, "You pity the plant, for which you did not labor, nor did you make it grow, which came into being in a night and perished in a night. And should not I pity Nineveh, that great city, in which there are more than 120,000 persons who do not know their right hand from their left, and also much cattle?" (Jonah 4:10–11)*

God's Attachment

It is a fascinating conclusion to the book. Jonah had greatly rejoiced over the plant's presence—and became deeply sorrowful when it was removed. Now it's as if God is saying: *Jonah, your anger, let's discuss. You really couldn't have loved this plant all that much. You didn't work for it. You didn't cause it to be. It came as quickly as it went. I, however, have loved these people with real love. I planted them, made them, worked for them, and want to see them turn to me.*

If Jonah felt so strongly about a plant, how should God feel about an entire city of **120,000 persons who do not know their right hand from their left**? At first glance, those who don't know their right from their left sounds like little children, and there are certainly a few scholars who think that's what God is referencing. If that is the case, God is merely saying there are lots of people in Nineveh, and since he made and cares about people, he cares about Nineveh.

This perspective is helpful because many modern Christians castigate and even despise city life—but God loves cities because lots of people live there. And even though the Bible begins with stories about rebellious cities, by the end of the Old Testament and the beginning of the New, God's people are called to love and serve the cities of the world. And, at the end of the Bible, when future events are depicted, God's people are gathered to his holy city forever. So perhaps all God is saying here is that he loves the city of Nineveh because he loves people.

But, in even the Bible itself, the phrase "do not know their right from their left" was a Hebrew idiom that meant "to distinguish or discriminate between certain things." For instance, it is used to describe an elderly man who could not taste or distinguish good food anymore or priests who weren't teaching people to discern between clean and unclean things (2 Samuel 19:35, Ezekiel 22:26, 44:23). Since God used the same idiom here, he *seems to be indicating that Nineveh has many people who are entrapped in sinful lifestyles and don't know how to get out.*[3]

They are certainly not morally innocent or somehow not responsible for their choices—that's why Jonah appeared with the word of judgment in the first place—but they are a confused and imprisoned people, a product of their time and culture. And God had **pity** on them (11). It is a word that indicates attachment. Jonah was attached to the plant, but that was an involuntary response because he needed shade while under the scorching desert sun. He was attached to the plan because the plant provided a service to him.

But God is unlike us—he is without a need of any kind. He doesn't even need our love—because he is Triune, perfect love has flowed from eternity past within himself. But God *chooses* to pity, *chooses* to attach himself, *chooses* to love. Though he does not need us, he loves us.

And God's question here at the close of the story is a searching one: Do we think of people as stuck in and blinded by sin? Do we see them in need of rescue and of much worth because—as God said of the Ninevites—God made them? Or do we see people as enemies? Do we gloat when they fail or ridicule them when we watch their actions? To behave like this is merely a way to detach like a coward from the people God is trying to rescue. It's merely self-protectionism, a pattern of disengagement, a way to feel morally superior and—like Jonah—safeguard your own.

Remember, God saw the evil of Nineveh more than Jonah did. And he sent his prophet right into that mess, but not with instruction and education on how to turns things around morally. Jonah wasn't there to give a lost and blind people training on how to live a righteous life. Instead, God sent Jonah with a message that was designed to get them to throw themselves on God's mercy—*perhaps he will relent!*

And God sends us in a similar way—not with moral training in an attempt to reform humanity from the outside in—but with a gospel message that has the potential to change people from the inside out.

On a recent flight, my seat was next to a man with a major snoring problem. He snored in a way that made other passengers turn to find where the sound was coming from—and in a way that made me worried he wasn't going to make it! It got so loud and violent at one point that I couldn't stop myself from chuckling. That's when the man on the other side of me told me that it was his boss, that he was on a business trip with a few other people, and that the man had been snoring like that all week. But no one knew what to tell him. For a second, I wondered if I was the man for the job.

But God had no such problem diagnosing and addressing Jonah's previously unknown issue. Jonah had not represented God well throughout his story, and this concluding question from God was like a sleep study designed to show Jonah the truth.

So the book of Jonah concludes with a searching question—one we hope eventually resonated with Jonah, and one we need today. Are our loves in the right order? Do we care deeply about lost humanity? More than we care about our own comforts? As I said, searching questions.

The Better Jonah

And the answers to those questions might discourage us. We might feel like modern Jonahs, at times misrepresenting God's nature to our world. Fortunately, Jesus came as the better than Jonah (and us). All the Old Testament heroes pointed to the better hero, one without any imperfection whatsoever, and Jonah is no exception. Jesus came from the Father and—as the Son of God and God the Son—he flawlessly represented God's heart. Jonah had little grace for people who didn't know their moral right from their left, but Jesus, while dying on the cross, prayed, *"Father, forgive them, for they know not what they do"* (Luke 23:34).

And all throughout his life and ministry, Jesus accurately showed us who God is, so much so that Hebrews calls him the *radiance of the glory of God and the exact imprint of his nature* (Hebrews 11:3).

But Jesus is also the figure who helps us solve our theological riddles. I mean, we should not be too dismissive of Jonah's quandary—he had a hard time seeing how God's grace was compatible with God's justice. And, though he was willing to accept God's grace for himself, he struggled when God extended that grace to the evil Ninevites.

If God was willing to extend mercy towards them, who in the world would he judge? And if God is also holy and righteous, isn't there a limit to his mercy and grace? And isn't justice and judgment needed, especially for those who are such a threat to others?

And, as our book ends, Jonah is still grappling with these questions about God. Just as the older brother stood dumbfounded when his father recklessly ran to his returning prodigal son, Jonah was still dumbfounded by God.

And we might expect moments where we also struggle with similar questions about God. But we have a better vantage point than Jonah because God's holiness and mercy, justice and grace are perfectly demonstrated in the cross of Christ. His cross is the one place where God completely extends his perfect love and total holiness. In the cross, God is not merely in total balance (he is always in total balance) but is totally expressed.

- How loving is God? Look at the cross—he loved you so much that he sent his only Son to die for you.

- How holy is God? Look at the cross—he is so perfect and pure that even one sin keeps us from his presence.

- How gracious and merciful is God? Look at the cross—he is so gracious that he gives himself to take our punishment.

- And how just is God? Look at the cross—he is so just that he does not dismiss even one ounce of the penalty for sin but instead consumed the entire penalty of wrath on that cross.

And now we all, Ninevites and Jonahs, must accept God's gift so that we can become his. To reject such a gift would be a sin worse than all others.

---

1. Ortlund, Dane C. 2021. Gentle and Lowly: The Heart of Christ for Sinners and Sufferers. Wheaton, IL: Crossway Books.
2. Keller, Timothy. 2018. The Prodigal Prophet: Jonah and the Mystery of God's Mercy. Viking.
3. Estelle, Bryan D. 2005. Salvation through Judgment and Mercy: The Gospel According to Jonah. Phillipsburg, NJ: P & R Publishing.

Bibliography

Barker, Kenneth L., and John R. Kohlenberger III. 2019. *The Expositor's Bible Commentary the Expositor's Bible Commentary: Old & New Testaments*. USA: Zondervan Academic.

Bruce, F. F. 1986. *New International Bible Commentary: With the New International Version*. Grand Rapids, MI: Zondervan.

Bruckner, James. 2010. *Jonah, Nahum, Habakkuk, Zephaniah*. Kentwood, MI: Zondervan.

Estelle, Bryan D. 2005. *Salvation through Judgment and Mercy: The Gospel According to Jonah*. Phillipsburg, NJ: P & R Publishing.

Keller, Timothy. 2018. *The Prodigal Prophet: Jonah and the Mystery of God's Mercy*. Viking.

Redmond, Eric, William Curtis, and Ken Fentress. 2016. *Exalting Jesus in Jonah, Micah, Nahum, Habakkuk*. Edited by David Platt, Daniel L. Akin, and Tony Merida. Holman Reference.

Rydelnik, Michael, and Michael Vanlaningham, eds. 2014. *The Moody Bible Commentary*. Chicago, IL: Moody Press.

Stewart, Douglas. 1987. *Hosea-Jonah. Vol. 31*. Dallas: Word Incorporated.

Walton, John H. 1982. *Jonah: A Bible Study Commentary*. Grand Rapids, MI: Zondervan.

Walvoord, and Zuck. 2003. *Bible Knowledge Commentary - the Old Testament*. Colorado Springs, CO: Victor Books.

About Nate

Nate Holdridge has served as senior pastor of Calvary Monterey on California's central coast since 2008. Calvary's vision is to see Jesus Famous. Nate teaches and writes with that aim at nateholdridge.com.

Nate also leads the Jesus Famous Podcast, conducting interviews and discussions that help us keep Jesus first. He has also written *The No-Nonsense Biblical Man*, *Dear New Dad*, *Whole-Hearted Work*, *(un)Reasonable Faith*, and more. Nate also serves as a member of the Executive Team of the Calvary Global Network.

He and Christina have been happily married since 2002, and are the proud parents of three incredible daughters.

Books

The No-Nonsense Biblical Man

Dear New Dad: An Introduction To Fatherhood

Let Us Hear: Studies on the Seven Letters of Revelation 2-3

Christ Unites: The Book Of Ephesians—How Jesus Connects His People To His Purpose

Whole-Hearted Work: Does My Work Matter To God? Can My Work Please God?

(un)Reasonable Trust: The Book of Habakkuk

Podcasts

Jesus Famous Podcast

Through The Bible Series Podcasts

Calvary Monterey Podcast